Sweden

A SMALL PORTRAIT OF A SMALL COUNTRY

SCANDINAVIAN FILM GROUP AS

This book is all about the Swedish nation. It aims to present a small portrait of a small, but also somewhat unusual country.

An unusually beautiful country, as people often tell us Swedes, which is satisfying, since we often think so ourselves too. We believe the best thing about Sweden is the country itself. At the same time, we feel able to share it with others. Gently, tastefully and in small portions. Glimpses from here and there, showing what it's like, what might be worth stopping to look at, and a little of what we get up to.

Of course, we too may need a small reminder of what we possess and how we want things to be in our country. Then there is more chance of it remaining that way, of it continuing to appear as it does in this book.

So that we don't wake up one day wondering what has happened to the dream.

Magnus Rietz
Editor

Contents

Stockholm

CITY OF NORDIC LIGHT

The sailing ship of Chapman lies moored at Skeppsholmen, opposite the Royal Palace, her white hull reflected in the water.

The traditional archipelago boats etch their V-shaped bow wave in the calm surface as they leave Blasieholmen quay. The Djurgården ferry plies back and forth between Djurgården and Slussen. To the west, the arch of Västerbron bridges the sparkling waters of Lake Mälaren.

Looking west, we also see the City Hall where the Nobel Prize ceremonies are held every December. To the east, towards the open sea, a string of green islands lines the shipping route into Stockholm. In the centre of the picture, the Old Town with its medieval lanes, cluster of roofs and centuries-old houses, their beautiful historic façades facing the water. From quaysides and boats anglers fish for sea trout or Baltic herring.

Gamla Stan, Stockholm's Old Town seen from Stadshustornet, the tower of Stockholm City Hall. Most of the buildings on this island, the original site of Stockholm, have survived intact from the seventeenth century.

Stockholm, the capital of Sweden, is built on about ten rocky islands at the point where the great Lake Mälaren flows into the Baltic. The city by the water is famous for its beauty and is sometimes called the Venice of the North, sometimes the Queen of Lake Mälaren. These may sound like clichés, but it is perfectly true that on a summer evening in June, when the bright northern sky is a bluish pink and a warm wind caresses the new leaves on the trees, Stockholm is heart-rendingly beautiful.

The view described is that from Mosebacke-terrassen in the Södermalm district, a stone's throw from Slussen. This is where Sweden's greatest author, August Strindberg, found inspiration for the opening scene of his novel The Red Room, which aroused great excitement on its publication in 1879 and subsequently became a classic.

The people standing on this spot in 1628 were

Old Town, Köpmanbrinken.
Just around the corner to the left you can travel
back in time in the seventeenth century vaulted
cellar restaurant, Diana.

able to observe the drama as the man-of-war Wasa sank off Beckholmen. Now the vessel is on display in a museum, not far from where she sank.

Today, the best views are to be had from the top of Katarinahissen, a public lift ascending the cliff face a few minutes' walk from Mosebacke. This is an excellent starting point for a city walk. Instead of taking the lift, we descend from the heights of Södermalm on foot via Urvädersgränd, a cobbled lane where the 18th-century troubadour poet Carl Michael Bellman once lived.

Slussen, the narrow stretch of water where Lake Mälaren meets the Baltic, can be crowded in summer with pleasure craft making their way out to the archipelago. Slussen is also the site of an ingenious traffic system, a manifestation of functionalism in the heart of the city. When Sweden switched to right-hand traffic in 1967, the split-level round-

The city skyline is at its best at dusk.
For a few weeks around midsummer the night sky is a
clear blue and late night revellers see Stockholm
in a whole new light.

about was shown to work as effectively as it had when people drove on the left.

Walking towards Gamla Stan (the Old Town), we have Mälaren on our left. Far to the west, on the shores of this great lake, lies the Viking settlement of Birka, where archaeological excavations have yielded finds from the 9th and 11th centuries ad.

Sweden's Royal Family also lives beside Lake Mälaren, in Drottningholm Palace, destination for many enjoyable excursions by traditional steamer.

The Old Town, or the City between the bridges, is the historic heart of Stockholm. In the 12th century, this strategically situated island contained only modest fortifications. A hundred years later, in the mid-13th century, Birger Jarl founded the city which became known as Stockholm. From the 16th century onwards, Stockholm acquired increasing importance as an administrative centre, and a stroll

through Gamla Stan is a walk through history from the 13th century to the present day. Gamla Stan is also home to the Royal Palace, large parts of which are open to the public.

The Swedish Academy, which awards the Nobel Prize for Literature, is based at Börshuset (the Old Stock Exchange). Its members sometimes dine at the historic Gyldene Freden tavern on Järntorget, a meeting place for Stockholm's poets since the 18th century. The city centre is a short walk from Gamla Stan, and nature is also close at hand. Djurgården forms part of Stockholm's unique urban national park, Ekoparken, which extends as far as Haga on the northern edge of the city.

To the east, the archipelago awaits you with its tens of thousands of islands.
For a taster, visit Fjäderholmarna, a 20-minute boat trip from Slussen.

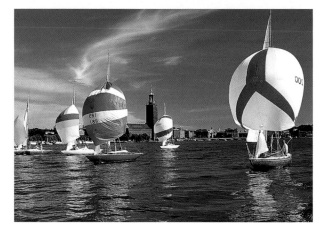

*Some of Stockholm's unique attractions - the Vasa Ship Museum, fishing at Strömmen,
sailing on Riddarfjärden and ballooning over the city centre on summer evenings.*

The most popular event of all - the Stockholm Water Festival. After a night-time fireworks display hundreds of boats make their way home across Riddarfjärden.

Inside the Globe Arena. The stadium hosts everything from ice hockey matches to rock concerts, from Lucia celebrations to boat shows.

The Stockholm archipelago

This great archipelago is unique, with its firths and sounds, its winding waterways between thousands of islands and skerries. The total number has been put at 24,000.

Closest to the mainland, the inner archipelago consists of large, wooded islands. Further out, in the central archipelago, the islands become smaller, and the waters more interspersed with islets and submerged rocks.

Furthest out, in the outer archipelago where the open sea begins, the islands are low-lying, the skerries bare, and the vegetation huddles in the crevices, seeking shelter from the wind. This is where the seals, seabirds and sea eagles dwell.

Out here, people count for little and are guaranteed safe passage only in calm weather. But on glorious summer days, this is where people always long to be, amid the silence, the splendour, the sunlight that comes from the east and sparkles in the waves rippling over the sea. In our grandparents' time, however, this summer paradise was quite different.

A June night at Högskär, Arholma.

The outer skerries were a tough workplace for the population of the islands nearer the mainland, who used to row or sail out here for a few weeks to fish for herring, which were then salted away. This provided them with an important addition to their staple diet and a tradable commodity which allowed them to purchase goods they were unable to produce themselves.

Men and women both took part in the work, living in small huts. In the long run, people found it impossible to sustain themselves by crofting, fishing and hunting. In the 1950s and 60s, the population of the archipelago fell by half. Even young people from the central archipelago moved to the mainland. Schools and post offices were closed. But in recent years, the trend of depopulation has been reversed, and the village schools have attracted more pupils. People earn their living in the traditional rural manner, by turning their hand to anything and being inventive. New technology has generated employment in the archipelago. If you phone your insurance company, the person answering may well be on Möja, one of the larger islands in the central archipelago. Tourists and summer visitors are a vital source of income for the archipelago's residents. Shops, restaurants and craftsmen do a roaring trade in summer. The traditional white archipelago boats are a much-loved feature of life in Stockholm's archipelago, having carried people and goods between the islands for over a century.

The archipelago extends for 150 km along the coast from north to south, while the distance from central Stockholm to the easternmost point, Svenska Högarna, a former lighthouse and pilot station, is 80 km as the crow flies. You could spend your whole lifetime sailing here and still not manage to see everything.

Svenska Högarna - the outermost
of all the island groups in Stockholm's archipelago.
One day in early June each year a long procession of
Stockholm's vintage steamers sails out to Vaxholm.
Lunch on the jetty - Swedish summer on a plate.

Approximately 400 boats take part in the Round Gotland Race, one of the world's largest offshore races, which brings Sandhamn to a standstill for a couple of days in early July each year. But on 1 January there aren't too many sailors about. Only the Vaxholm ferry Skarpö runs this far out.

*The fastest boats in the Round Gotland Race round the island
and cross the finish line in just over two days.*

The Vaxholm ferry Storskär is the king of the archipelago's steamers.
At thirteen knots you can stand on deck and watch jetties, islands and inlets gently sweeping by.

The South

SMÅLAND, ÖLAND, SKÅNE AND BLEKINGE

Småland is situated in the middle of Southern Sweden and, contrary to what its name suggests, it is the largest province in Götaland. Its name originates from when several "small districts" or communities united in the middle ages to form this rich and varied landscape.

The uplands in the north-west of Småland undulate with their deep valleys. Southern Sweden's highest point is at Tomtabacken, 378 metres above sea level. The uplands are hit by the humid winds from the Atlantic, and this extremely rainy and snowy climate differs markedly from the low coastline in the east which is sheltered from the rain.

Småland offers a variety of nature and different landscapes. Vast forests, peaceful lakes, varied agricultural landscapes, open coastline and skerries.

Houses in Småland are part of the landscape like nowhere else in Sweden.

The timber industry has long been of great importance here in Småland, Southern Sweden's most abundantly wooded region. Furniture and ready-to-assemble timber houses are a couple of examples. Nowadays, the most internationally renowned products are probably the pieces of furniture from IKEA which you assemble yourself.

In the past, safety matches were exported worldwide from the mid-19th century onwards. Småland's enterprising nature is legendary.

Alongside major companies such as Huskvarna, the smaller industries around Gnosjö have kept going even through times of economic hardship.

Numerous stone walls and boundary marks in the agricultural landscape recall the unceasing labours of the farmers to enlarge the cultivable areas in the stony south-east of Småland. Their labours were not enough to feed everyone, and in the middle of last century there was a mass exodus to America. The record year was 1882, when over 50 000 Swedes emigrated to the larger country on the other side of the Atlantic.

At 6 km, the Öland bridge is the longest in Sweden.

Högby lighthouse on Öland is the home of artist Stephan Lundh where he paints, fishes and dives for wrecks. Hundreds of ships have been wrecked along the east coast of Öland, including the warship Kronan, found outside Segerstad in 1980. She was wrecked in 1676 in a naval battle with the Danish-Dutch fleet. Many artefacts from the wreck are now in Kalmar County Museum.

The writer Vilhelm Moberg described this era in a series of books which were made into a film, and also a musical written by the former members of the pop group ABBA, Benny Andersson and Björn Ulvaeus.

In these parts, there are places that are famous throughout the world for their quality glassware and crystal, such as Kosta, Boda and Orrefors. This is glass-making country with traditions dating back to the 18th century. Many of the glassworks have closed down, but a trip round the glass factories in this smiling landscape is still a must for the visitor. From here it is not far to öland, the special island beside the straits of Kalmar.

If you're travelling from Småland's glass-making country or Öland to Österlen in Skåne, you can easily pass through Blekinge in a couple of hours. But it is worth stopping off in this little region with such rich, luxuriant vegetation that it is known as the garden of Sweden. Forests and lakes, skerries and cliffs, beaches and sea — Blekinge is Sweden in miniature, with all these close at hand. Protected by

Sweden's southernmost archipelago lies the ancient naval city of Karlskrona, which has long been of strategic importance, particularly during Sweden's days as a great power in the 17th century.

Öland

"We hardly touched the beaches of Öland, until we noticed that this countryside was completely different from the other Swedish provinces."

That was observed by Carl von Linné, Sweden's world-famous naturalist, "the floral king", on his visit to Öland in 1741. The same observation is nowadays made by everyone who drives across the mighty bridge over the straits of Kalmar to visit öland for the first time. Southern Öland is dominated by Stora Alvaret, an expanse of limestone, where the vegetation has been kept down by animals grazing over hundreds of years, an unparalleled kind of nature.

An open landscape, punctuated with the odd

Ölandsgård, Långlöt.

Blåeld, Neptuni Åkrar, Öland.
In the background is the island Blå Jungfrun in the
centre of Kalmar sound, a national park and, as
legend has it, a landing place for witches.

bush, almost flat but with slight, hardly perceptible changes in height. Stora Alvaret does not offer an instant, dramatic experience of nature. It is an unobtrusive landscape, but if you give it time, stroll over it, Alvaret offers a prehistoric, almost magical experience.

All around there are memories of our fore-fahers. Öland's history dates back nearly 10 000 years, and ancient hill forts are clearly visible in the landscape. For those interested in botany, Alvaret is a centre of pilgrimage in early summertime.

The characteristic flower, Öland's rockrose, en-chants with its dense carpet of resplendent yellow petals, and all the orchids greatly impressed even in Linné's time.

The southern point of Öland with its lighthouse, Långe Jan, is strategically situated as a resting place on the flight path of migratory birds. Here you can see species which are not found elsewhere in Swe-den, and there is also an ornithological station where the birds are tagged and research is carried out on migratory birds.

Sandhammaren, Skåne - the southeasternmost corner of Sweden and home to the country's finest sandy beaches.

Skåne

Sweden's southernmost province. Since the old days it has been known as the granary of Sweden. In the southernmost parts, cultivation takes up most of the flat landscape.

In this agricultural district, the landscape looks like a multi-coloured patchwork quilt from above. The patches of the quilt are arable fields of different colours depending on which crops grow there. The results of the labours of cultivation are so attractive that they feature in Swedish literature. A classic among the descriptions of the Skåne people's eating and drinking habits is Fritiof Nilsson Piraten's book *Bock i Örtagård.* Of course, extravagant menus of food and drink can be enjoyed in many places, but perhaps ideally in Skåne's traditional inns.

Skåne has a continental feel to it. Once it belonged to Denmark, until the Treaty of Roskilde in 1658, and is densely populated by Swedish standards.

Although Skåne is often associated with flat agricultural countryside, the region includes various types of scenery and is certainly not completely flat. In the north, towards the border with Småland, there are large forests. Skåne's long coast is lined with picturesque fishing villages and long sandy beaches, but is also quite steep in places.

In the east is the rolling countryside known as Österlen, known primarily for its apple orchards, and popular with artists, authors and holidaymakers. Ancient monuments, castles and stately homes abound in Skåne.

The cities of Malmö and Helsingborg on the west coast are Sweden's gateways to the continent.

TOP: *Brösarp hills in Österlen. Drive slowly and enjoy the undulating countryside and twisting roads.*
BOTTOM: *In the winter driving in Skåne isn't quite as much fun.*
The snow falls wherever it likes and drifts several metres high are not uncommon.

Helsingborg harbour is the gateway to the continent.
TOP LEFT: *Ystad, an ancient town with the old terraced houses typical of Skåne.*
TOP RIGHT: *Classic farm in Skåne.* BOTTOM LEFT: *Field of rape in Österlen - the golden oil of Skåne.*
BOTTOM RIGHT: *Mölle at Kullaberg - one of the first fashionable bathing resorts in Sweden.*

The changing face of the countryside of southern Sweden.
Hovs Hallar, Bjärehalvön. View over the Öresund.

Hills at Brösarp, Österlen. Willow walk, Svenstorp.

The WestCoast

CLIFFS OF GRANITE , TOURISTS AND SMALL FISHING VILLAGES

Bohuslän is Sweden's Atlantic seaboard, beyond it the Skagerrak, the North Sea and the wide world. The prevailing wind here is from the west, and on stormy days the waves have a clear run all the way from the British Isles, as much of the flotsam and jetsam washed ashore goes to show.

Here is where the last, bare offshoots of Scandinavia's mountain backbone meet the sea, creating a particularly varied landscape. Nearest the coast, barren, weatherbeaten rocks, the granite growing redder the further north you go. Tightly pressed against the hillsides, sheltered from the wind, stand the typical white-painted farmhouses. Many artists have found inspiration in this landscape of contrasts, and the special light produced by the combination of briny sea, mountains and soil. Not to mention the bathers, tourists and yachtsmen who have been flocking here since the late 19th century.

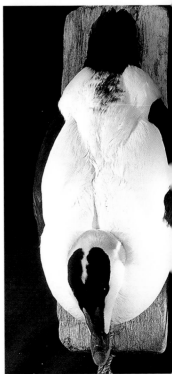

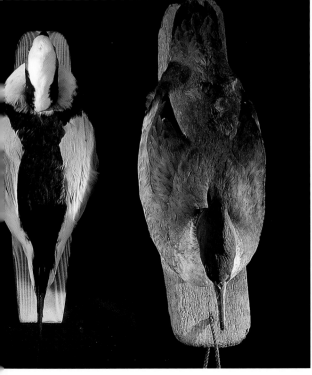

Standing on the shore looking out to sea during the summer, you can see a chain of sails on the horizon like a pearl necklace. The flag flying in the stern of each boat is usually Swedish, Danish, Norwegian, German or Dutch.

Starting just north of Vinga, the navigable channel up the coast of Bohuslän is so busy with yachting traffic in summer that it is jestingly called the sea's E6, referring to the European Highway that traverses Bohuslän from the port city of Gothenburg to the Norwegian border at Svinesund.

Vinga, a tiny rocky skerry, is where Evert Taube grew up as a lighthouse keeper's son at the end of last century. He became one of Sweden's most popular troubadour poets, and his works are the foremost depictions of Bohuslän in words, music and pictures. The region's fishing villages, seafaring communities and coastal waters, and not least its people, all feature in his poetry and songs. Taube's ballads typify the romanticism of the Swedish skerries, whether on the west or the east coast.

As Vinga vanishes behind us, the popular island of Marstrand with its fortress comes into view. Marstrand's tradition as a bathing resort dates back to the 19th century, when King Oscar II was the most prominent visitor. Nowadays it is a major yachting centre.

The next large island, Orust, is Sweden's third largest, and is famous for its boatbuilding, forests and agriculture.

If calmer waters appeal to you, the narrow channels surrounding Flatön and Bassholmen, where boat enthusiasts can be seen restoring traditional vessels, offer a truly idyllic experience.

From the resort of Fiskebäckskil, a ferry plies to and fro across the Gullmarsfjord to the town of Lysekil, where at Havets Hus you can study the marine life, which is particularly abundant here by

Old fishing villages are now sought
after by summer residents. Tjörnekalv off Tjörn.
A traditional wooden motor boat.
NEXT PAGE: *In the middle of Bohuslän*
about level with Lysekil, the rocks turn from red
to grey. Hållö outside Smögen.

Swedish standards. You can have even more fun if you don a skin-diver's mask and explore beneath the surface as you take a dip. Amid the swirling seaweed, you may catch sight of a brightly coloured cuckoo wrasse or some other funnily named fish.

Just north of Lysekil, the chiselled form of Bohus Malmön reminds us that quarrying was once a major industry alongside fishing, agriculture and boatbuilding. Buildings made of Bohus granite are found all over the world: around the Arc de Triomphe in Paris, and along the waterfront in Buenos Aires and Havana. Continuing north, we pass the Fjällbacka skerries and enter Kosterrännan, the channel running between the Koster islands and Strömstad. Kosterrännan is Sweden's only maritime environment with species that are otherwise found only in deep waters. Just south of Strömstad is Tjärnö Marine Research Laboratory, where scientists study this rich submarine world. In summer you can view the aquatic life at various depths in Tjärnö aquarium.

Together with their colleagues at Lysekil and Fiskebäckskil, the scientists at Tjärnö also monitor threats to the sensitive marine environment.

To the east, a short distance inland, the long, narrow Bullare lakes and the Kynnefjäll hills offer a magical experience of nature. There are many legends of strange goings-on in these parts, and in the old days numerous villains are said to have taken refuge from the law in these great forests. Tanum is home to 3 000-year-old rock carvings from the Bronze Age, now a World Heritage Site. Experts differ as to exactly what Bohuslän's prehistoric inhabitants were trying to express, but it is possible to identify themes such as fertility, hunting, power, conflict and a form of religion — in short, the same sort of things we make films and TV programmes about nowadays ...

Väderöbod lighthouse is a barren outpost in the Skagerak. The lighthouse was manned until the 1960s and staff used to be paid a loneliness bonus.
NEXT PAGE: *The island of Åstol outside Tjörn. Just why all these houses were built on top of each other down the cliff is a secret lost in the mists of time.*

The fruits of the sea are on sale at bargain prices in Smögen.' An evening walk on the jetty for the shrimp auction is one of the highlights of summer.

Tjörn Runt - this round-island race held in August each year attracts hundreds of boats and even more spectators for a party on the rocks.

Swedish houses

FROM CASTLES TO COTTAGES

Many Swedes still dream of owning a red cottage with white window frames, which has become synonymous with the countryside, summertime and holidays.

Preferably it should be built of wood and painted red with white window frames, perhaps with a gabled, tiled roof and a small garden with a lilac bower. Add a few birch trees close by, a flagpole, and the dream is complete.

The red Swedish cottage.

Golden ochre is a traditional shade used on the facades of finer buildings, such as Sillegården in Värmland.

In the 18th century it became fashionable to paint houses with Falu rödfärg, a special kind of red paint whose pigment is a by-product from the copper mine at Falun.

Although it was originally a question of fashion, the thick red paint also turned out to be an effective rot-proofing agent and is still regarded as superior to modern plastic paints. Anyone travelling through the Swedish countryside will notice that the red paint from Falun is used throughout the country.

In a country with as many forests as Sweden, it is only natural for houses to be built of wood. In this coniferous region, pine timber was the obvious raw material. The tradition known as knuttimring, a method of dovetailing the logs at the corners, goes back to Viking times. An eldhus ("fire house") was a one-room dwelling with a hearth at its centre and a hole in the middle of the roof to let the smoke out. Later, people discovered how to build better fireplaces with chimneys, but the tradition of knuttimring survives to this day.

In places where deciduous trees grow, primarily in southern Sweden, a different technique is used: walls with a framework of vertical pillars interspersed with heavy oak planking.

A new house, mass-produced and ready to assemble, complete with tower.
Home builders in Sweden are increasingly using romanticism and charm to attract buyers.

In the old days, houses built of masonry were unusual in rural areas, except on the islands of Öland and Gotland, where local stone was used. Stone buildings were more common in the towns, one reason being the risk of fire.

While country folk were able to get a good warm fire going in their small timber cottages, the aristocracy and royalty probably sat with their teeth chattering all winter in their big stone castles, so difficult to heat.

Sweden's many castles and stately homes remind us that the country was once a great power. The castles were built partly for defensive purposes,

but also to impress the rest of Europe, which is why Drottningholm Palace, for example, was made to rival Versailles in terms of size and decoration.

Sweden's first great castles were built in the mid-13th century during the reign of Birger Jarl, the founder of Stockholm.

Besides protecting against enemy attack, these medieval royal castles were meant to reinforce the king's power, enabling the various parts of the country to be governed.

Of the many castles built in the 16th century under King Gustav Vasa, several remain intact: Kalmar, Gripsholm, Uppsala and Vadstena. These castles

Läckö Castle on Lake Vänern, one of the most magnificent castles from Sweden's days as a great power.
Built by Magnus Gabriel de la Gardie in the 17th century and still a major tourist attraction.
1. Drottningholm, the royal residence. 2. Sundby Castle. 3. Vrams Gunnarstorp.
4. Hjularöds Castle. 5. Kalmar Castle. 6. China pavilion, Lovö Island.

1

3

2

4

5

6

1. *The manor houses of Hälsingland were often built by arrogant landowners to impress their neighbours during the 18th and 19th centuries.* 2. *This little house, Snoppebo on Huvudskär in the Stockholm archipelago, is built mainly from driftwood.* 3. *Nowadays you can buy prefabricated summerhouses at every DIY store. Ideally a summerhouse should be beside water.* 4. *A shepherd's hut in Härjedalen. These days, such huts are occupied only by holidaymakers and the occasional hillwalker.*

served the same purpose as the medieval fortresses.

During Sweden's days as a great power in the 17th century, the aristocracy practically competed with the royal family to show off its wealth and power. Skokloster, Läckö and Tidö are examples of castles built as the residences of powerful aristocrats.

Stockholm's old castle, Tre Kronor (Three Crowns), was destroyed by fire at the end of the 17th century. As a result, the present Royal Palace was designed, which with 600 rooms is the largest in Scandinavia.

Between the two architectural extremes, castles and cottages, there is an astonishing variety of house types, ranging from austere Functionalism to highly ornamented timber creations.

It is also worth noting how well older houses are situated in the countryside. In Sweden's relatively harsh climate, people often built their houses on south-facing slopes for maximum sunlight, some way up the slope to avoid the frost down in the valley, and preferably with some trees at the top of the hill to protect against the north-westerly wind.

Gotland

A UNIQUE ISLAND

Gotland, the largest island in the Baltic, first appears as a narrow strip on the horizon. Soon you see the bright, steep cliffs of the island's west coast, but not until going ashore do you appreciate the magic of this place. Gotland is unique.

The sense of going back in time is strong in the medieval Hanseatic town of Visby with its characteristic town walls, cobbled streets, ruined churches and picturesque little houses and lanes.

Some visitors to Gotland are so captivated by Visby that they spend the rest of their holiday in its unique historic surroundings. Inside its 13th-century walls, the town is effectively one large ancient monument that justly deserves its status as a Unesco World Heritage Site.

Visby town walls were built in the thirteenth century and are the largest man-made structure in Sweden. Careful renovation is still underway.

At the height of summer, the lanes bustle with activity. Many young people visit Visby, and the restaurants, cafés and pubs are packed out. If it gets too hot, the sea is always close at hand.

Many people prefer the calmer pace of life in Visby after the peak tourist season lasting from Midsummer until mid-August. Autumn is mild on the island, and well into October you can still enjoy

warm days as a result of the heat stored up by the sea over the summer.

But for most visitors, Gotland is a summer island with a distinctive landscape. The limestone rocks with their special flora, including rare orchids, the beauty of Gotland's blossoming meadows, the beaches, the crags, the sun and the sea — in this open landscape you can find peace of mind. You have the

illusion of being much further south, in the Mediterranean almost. The coastal climate means the island enjoys many more hours of sunshine than most other places in Sweden.

Gotland offers a wide variety of nature. From the barren beauty of Fårö in the north to idyllic seaside fields where cattle graze, flowering meadows, pine woods, lakes and innumerable beaches, each with

The second week in August each year is Medieval Week on Gotland, where Visby is transformed into a fourteenth century Hanseatic town. Valdemar Atterdag of Denmark threatens to burn the town once more just as in 1361. Thousands of people dress up as everything from beggars to knights for a week-long festival of parties, jousting and markets. This is possibly Sweden's most popular event and attracts visitors from all over Europe.

its own character. From finest sand to cobblestones. Agriculture is characterised by grazing sheep, Gotland's traditional symbol.

The island's coasts abound in bird life. Several areas are closed off during the breeding season in spring and early summer, but there are plenty of birdwatching towers.

Gotland is cycling country, with many beautiful roads running beside the sea, and others traversing the island's age-old agricultural landscape. History and culture are never far from the beaten track.

The numerous stone churches are a monument to Gotland's glory days in the early 12th century, and many of them contain major artistic treasures. Tumuli and cairns from the Bronze Age, burial grounds from the Iron Age and hill forts from the

centuries immediately following Christ's birth recall Gotland's inhabitants through the ages.

Artists have always been attracted to Gotland by the special light from the sea and the limestone, the sense of past meeting present and the island's unique nature.

However, a true picture of this landscape of light can linger only in the memory.

Open, often moor-like countryside largely populated by sheep is Gotland at its most typical. Barshageudd, the southernmost tip of the island.
TOP: *The houses on the island are often built of limestone, The style of building is very traditional and is unique to Gotland.*
NEXT PAGE: *Located in the middle of the sea, Gotland has no archipelago. The sea begins where the land ends. Boats are just pulled up the shingle beaches out of the waves.*

Traditional interiors of houses on Gotland. These are historical interiors between a hundred and three hundred years old in style. While new houses on Gotland hardly look like this any more, home furnishing magazines from all four corners of the world send journalists to Gotland to report on this phenomenon over and over again.

NEXT PAGE: *Groddagården in Fleringe, northwest Gotland.*
Langhammars stone pillars, Fårö. These stone pillars were once carved out by the sea.
Although very old they are easily damaged so don't go climbing!

Dalarna

HOME OF SWEDISH ROMANTICISM

For generations, Dalarna has been considered to embody the essence of all things Swedish, with its living traditions such as Midsummer celebrations, fiddle music and peasant costumes.

The very name Dalarna (the Dales) sounds poetic, and the region certainly contains a rich variety of dales, mountains, lakes and hills.

At the turn of the last century, the artists Carl Larsson and Anders Zorn did much to foster the Swedish National Romantic movement, subsequently achieving international fame.

TOP: *Self-portrait by Anders Zorn, Dalarna's and possibly Sweden's foremost portrait painter of all time.*
RIGHT: *Midsummer, a church boat on Lake Siljan. Leksand peasant costumes, a mark of genuine Swedishness found only in Dalarna.*

TOP: *Fryksås, a byre in mid-winter.*
This is the idyllic winter scene in the country which
in real life exists only on Christmas cards.
BOTTOM: *There are many hundreds of regional and local*
variants of traditional costume in Sweden. There are also
customs and traditions as to how women should wear their
hair when wearing the costume: pinned up or loose, cove-
red or bare. Often a distinction is made between married
and unmarried women. The plait is optional, however.

Even in the early years of this century, Dalarna had begun to attract increasing numbers of visitors, the beginnings of mass tourism. Many travellers in those days saw Dalarna as one large folk museum. This aroused the anger of local people who were not prepared to behave like museum exhibits, culminating in 1918 in anti-tourist demonstrations in Rättvik. Prices were high, food was scarce, and priority had been given to tourists.

Nowadays visitors are made welcome in Dalarna, mass tourism being a key industry. Traditional culture such as fiddle-playing still flourishes, however.

Folk music has a life of its own. The Dalarna Fiddlers' Association has 1300 members, the largest such group in Sweden. The musicians play by ear, without music, passing on the tunes from generation to generation.

Some of the tunes have your legs itching to dance, others express the melancholy of the great forests. Fiddlers' rallies attract huge audiences from far and wide.

As early as the 1930s, tourists were being urged not only to visit the beautiful area around Lake Siljan, with its cherished cultural heritage, but to allow time to see the entire region. Because of its location where northern and southern Sweden meet, Dalarna is unique in terms of nature. From desolate moors in the north to fertile deciduous forests in the south, this is the northernmost limit for many species of flora and fauna. Alongside commercially important conifer plantations, you can see remnants of primeval forest, now protected. North of Orsa, you may meet the occasional bear.

Mining has played a central role in Dalarna's history. Iron ore in the mountains, forests and running water, the region had everything necessary for operating furnaces and smelters.

The southern parts, the Bergslagen dales, contain many monuments to the golden age of mining. A journey past some of the former smelters will really fire your imagination.

As well as iron ore, copper mining was also very important. The most obvious manifestation of Dalarna's products must be all the red-painted houses and barns in Sweden. The red paint used is a by-product from the copper mine at Falun, which began operations 1000 years ago, reaching its peak in the mid-17th century when Falun was Sweden's principal industrial town. Falun copper mine has now ceased production, but a preserved mine and museum remain open to visitors, and the manufacture of red paint continues.

Traditional costumes are a timeless fashion for young and old alike. Rättvik peasant costumes.

RIGHT: *The Vasa Run is a 90 km cross-country skiing contest attracting some 10,000 participants annually. Only a fraction of these are competing against one another, though. The vast majority are competing against themselves, struggling to reach their destination at all.*

TOP: *The women of Dalarna, known as kullor, have always played a prominent role. Anders Zorn had a predilection for painting Dala-women bathing. During the Vasa Run, for instance, attention is focused more on the leading woman than on the actual winner of the race.*

The Forest

AN ANCIENT PLACE OF REFUGE

The moss gleams succulent green in the sunlight streaming down between the branches of the fir trees. The bilberry and cowberry twigs rustle with your every step. Oh look, a chanterelle! Golden yellow, the delight of every mushroom picker.

A little stream ripples on its way. Silence prevails, the wind is but a faint rustle in the treetops, and on the barren slopes of the mountain, a woodpecker searches for food in an old twisted pine tree.

A while spent walking in the woods is the essence of life for every Swede. Even though not all Swedes take advantage of it regularly, this refuge is always at the back of their mind.

The manifold colours of autumn in the beech woods on the lower slopes. The very start of autumn, when all the colours are present simultaneously, is the most beautiful time.

The forests are every Swede's playground and, with few exceptions, you are never far from a woodland grove no matter whereabouts in Sweden you live. Over half the country's surface area is afforested, primarily with conifers.

The Swedes first meet the inhabitants and plants of the forest in fairytales and nursery rhymes. We sing of Mother's Little Olle who met a bear in the woods, of Putte whose lips turned bluish-red, like all children who eat bilberries, and of cowberry jam, an essential accompaniment to swedish pancakes.

In the forest you may well encounter deer, elk and woodland birds such as the capercaillie and black grouse, while further north you may meet the odd bear or wolf.

Nowadays not many forests resemble those of the fairytales, and completely unspoiled woodlands are rare even in Sweden. Since time immemorial the

The forest larder. Like berry picking, mushroom picking for personal consumption is free, being part of the Swedish tradition of unrestricted access to all land.

forests have provided us with wood for making fires and building houses, and with berries and mushrooms to gather.

Timber and pulp have long been one of Sweden's main exports. Ancient woodlands or remnants of primeval forest are becoming increasingly rare in the era of mechanised forestry.

Mass deforestation and plantation have replaced the old-fashioned methods of felling, reducing the number of species present in the forest. In recent years, however, increased environmental awareness has led forestry operators to begin taking an interest in biodiversity and refining their harvesting methods.

Some ancient woodlands have been given protected status. Even commercial forests offer a wealth of interesting nature if timber extraction is carefully managed.

The forest is Sweden's greatest natural resource. Unfortunately, emotional and biological interests often conflict with economic ones. To retain the enchanted forest while harvesting it is not easy, of course.

*Industrial forest, bog forest, primeval forest – the whole of Sweden is covered in forest, apart from
a few miles at each end of the country. However, the age and character of the trees varies noticeably.
Ramtorp, Sörmland. Njakafjäll, Lappland. Primeval forest, Stora Sjöfallet National Park*

Lapland

THE GREAT WILDERNESS

The thermometer reads 30 degrees below zero. The air is perfectly still, freezing fog shrouds the valleys, your breath turns to white frost in your hair and beard, and the smoke from the chimney of the lonely cottage rises vertically into the pink sky.

Europe's last wilderness. As far as the eye can reach, not a house, a road, a telephone wire to be seen. The sense of unspoilt nature is total. People come from all over the world to experience this feeling. To see the Northern Lights, the remarkable atmospheric phenomenon with shimmering green veils dancing high in the ionosphere on clear, cold winter nights, and the Midnight Sun, an equally memorable sight to marvel at during the summer.

Lapland in the middle of winter. It's cold – minus 30 to 40 degrees is nothing unusual. Knivkammen, Kebnekajse.

Not all of Swedish Lapland is wilderness by any means. Modern forestry methods are used in many places, numerous rivers and watercourses have been dammed to provide hydro-electric power, and snow scooters have made some inland regions more accessible — albeit only in winter.

Large parts of the landscape consist of seemingly endless, low-lying bog and forest land.

In the west, towards the Norwegian border, the countryside rises to form great mountains, Scandinavia's mountain backbone which runs south from here until it divides and plunges into the North Sea at its south-western extremity.

Forestry and mining have long been key industries in Northern Sweden. Export profits have helped generate prosperity. Sweden's hydro-electric power also comes primarily from the North. As in most other parts of the world, human exploitation of natural resources has left its mark, sometimes with irreparable consequences.

The true wilderness is found in the region's north-westernmost corner. This is Europe's largest single protected area, its nature virtually unspoilt. The Padjelanta, Sarek, Stora Sjöfallet and Muddus national parks, the Sjaunja and Stubba nature reserves, and Sulitelma, Tjuoltadal and Rapadelta — the

Lapp handicrafts and food from nature's larder.
Piolaslätten, Sarek National Park. Now listed by the
UN as a World Heritage Site.

A Lapp hut. The style of building has not changed significantly for centuries.
Nowadays people only live like this in the mountains.

Every reindeer is a four-legged moveable investment for the Lapps. Lack of grazing, road traffic, poachers and even wolves pose constant threats to their assets. The reindeer roam freely in the wild and are herded into pens only for marking and slaughter.

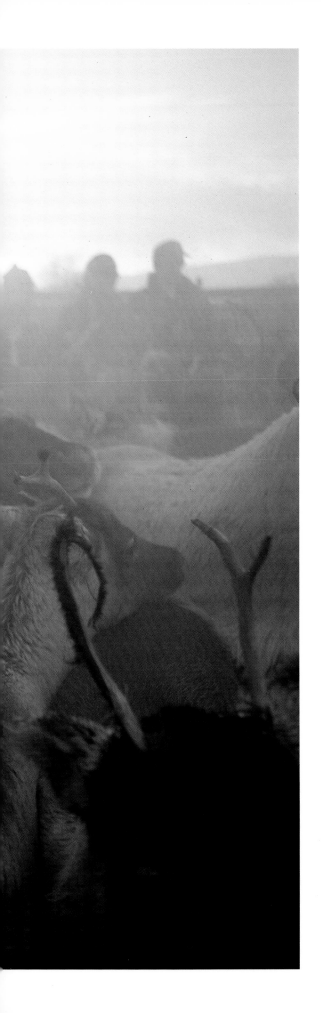

LEFT: *Separating the reindeer into herds in the autumn.*
TOP: *The Northern Lights, the winter atmospheric phenomenon. Six months later, it's the Midnight Sun which never sets.*
BOTTOM: *Potholing at Björkliden, where neither the Northern Lights nor the Midnight Sun penetrate, nor many tourists. Björkliden is better known for its good skiing above ground.*

area known as Laponia is so unique, thanks to its magnificent nature, abundant flora and fauna and historical significance to Lapp culture, that it has been designated a World Heritage Site by Unesco.

The area combines priceless natural and cultural heritage, containing everything from primeval forest and bog to steep mountains, glaciers and mighty waterfalls. Here you find bears, lynx, wolverines and the occasional wolf, though many wolves have migrated south in recent years.

In the skies above, golden eagles, sea eagles, buzzards and peregrine falcons are among the species keeping watch.

Laponia is also home to traditional Lapp culture. The oldest traces of human habitation date back over 7 000 years. These traces are not obvious, but they are there nonetheless.

Thousands of ancient pitfalls provide proof that Sweden's original inhabitants used to keep themselves by hunting wild reindeer.
Not until the 17th century did reindeer herding become the main activity of the Lapps.

Kebnekajse, southern summit.
In Sarek, you can walk for days or even weeks
on end without meeting anyone.

High days and holidays

THE HIGHLIGHTS OF THE YEAR

Skansen, the folk museum in Stockholm, is a collection of traditional rural buildings, traditions and festivals from all over Sweden. The Midsummer celebrations here are in keeping with the style.

Walpurgis Night, 30 April, at Örebro Castle. Bonfires of all sorts are lit throughout the country, ranging from piles of leaves to veritable rubbish heaps. People sing student songs and hail the arrival of spring.

A Whitsun wedding. You may need to book the church up to a year in advance.
A juice party in the bower, a highlight for the children, particularly on Midsummer Eve.

Midsummer celebrations in the country. Round dancing, games and folk music in the afternoon. Herring, new potatoes, strawberries and a dram. Midsummer Night follows – light, bright and possibly romantic if you're lucky on the dance floor.

Summer, summer, summer –
Sweden enjoys five weeks of statutory holiday, and spending some of it in your hammock is an established tradition.

Pickled herring is raw, fermented fish which, particularly in Northern Sweden, has been raised to the status of a cult and tradition. People either love this dish or beat a hasty retreat when the tin is opened and the smell wafts forth.

Throughout August, the summer warmth remains, but the evenings descend like a black veil. That's when the crayfish are caught in the lakes and rivers, boiled with lots of dill until deliciously red, and finally eaten amid special rituals. The shell must be removed, the syrup lapped up, and the various parts tasted and remarked upon together with schnapps, bread and cheese. All beneath the gleam of Chinese lanterns.

The dinner that everyone would like to attend, though few people are actually invited – the Nobel Prize ceremony in Stockholm City Hall in December. The crockery, food and service are legendary.

Lucia, the Queen of Light, is commemorated on 13 December. Accompanied by a singing procession, she and her attendants parade through homes and workplaces throughout Sweden, radiating light and beauty. Even the Nobel Prize winners, who are in Stockholm at this time of year, are usually awakened by a Lucia procession.

Christmas dinner on board the Stockholm archipelago boat Gustafsberg VII.
Any self-respecting Swedish company invites its staff and customers to a Christmas dinner in December.

Excursions
and sights

*Balloon trips over Stockholm operate every fine evening in summer,
but you need to book at least a couple of days in advance.*

The folk museum and zoo at Skansen on Djurgården includes all the Scandinavian animals.
The more exotic species are left to the travelling circuses that visit Stockholm in the summer.

The magnificent man-of-war Wasa foundered and sank before the watching eyes of Stockholm's citizens on her maiden voyage in 1628.

Not until 1961, when she was salvaged, did she re-emerge from the waters of Stockholms Ström. The Wasa Museum is open all year round.

*Market day during Gotland's Medieval Week in August, a very exciting event
which you should preferably don medieval dress to take part in.*

The Thousand Island Cruise – a full day's voyage from Stockholm to exciting islands on the edge of the open sea.
Ansgar's Chapel at Birka, an island in Lake Mälaren which was the largest Viking settlement in the Sweden of old.
The Hallwyl Palace in Stockholm. Ostentatious, ornamented and unbelievably extravagant.

It is possible to hire genuine log rafts and float slowly down the River Klarälven in Värmland. A trip on the Göta Canal is like travelling by boat through the countryside. The journey through the heart of Sweden takes three days.

Zorngården at Mora, where Anders Zorn, one of Sweden's greatest painters, had his studio in a 12th-century former bakehouse. A remarkable mixture of architectural styles, devised by the artist himself.

Our World Heritage

PLACES WORTH PRESERVING

Some places in the world are so precious that their preservation is the concern of all humanity. Such priceless treasures may be either cultural or natural.

The United Nations operates the World Heritage Convention, under which some 500 places across the globe are listed as World Heritage Sites. About ten of these are in Sweden.

AT TANUM in Bohuslän there are wonderful Bronze Age rock carvings, approximately 3,000 years old.

DROTTNINGHOLM PALACE by Lake Mälaren, also known as "Little Versailles", is a uniquely well-preserved palace, unusually large by Scandinavian standards.

BIRKA on the island of Björkö in Lake Mälaren was an important Viking trading centre in the Sweden of old.

SKOGSKYRKOGÅRDEN in Stockholm is an example of an entire architectural concept in strict Functionalism.

THE HANSEATIC CITY OF VISBY is a unique medieval environment with its well-preserved town walls.

ENGELSBERGS BRUK in Västmanland recalls the importance of the mining industry.

GAMMELSTADS KYRKSTAD in Luleå is a collection of small cottages where families who had to travel a long way used to stay when attending major church festivals.

LAPLAND WORLD HERITAGE SITE, the first World Natural Heritage Site in Scandinavia, is also a World Cultural Heritage Site for the Lapp people.

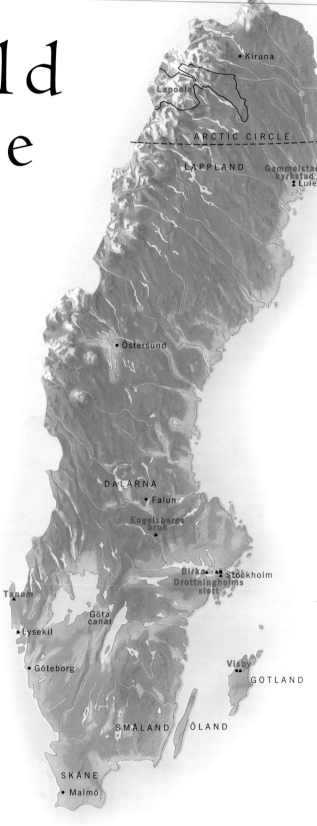

Population: 8.5 million. Area: 449,964 km2. North-south distance: 1,574 km. East-west distance: 499 km. Illustration: Hans Sjögren

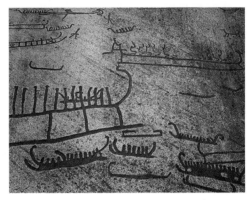

The Swedish Royal Family. Drottningholm Palace, Lake Mälaren. The Hanseatic City of Visby. Engelsbergs Bruk, Västmanland. The rock carvings at Tanum, Bohuslän. Gammelstads Kyrkstad, Luleå. Laponia, Scandinavia's first World Natural Heritage Site

Photographers
and picture sources

Per Erik Adamsson/Great Shots: 97. Rolf Adlercreutz/Tiofoto: 53 bl. Ragnar Andersson/Tiofoto: 70, 71, 74. Torbjörn Arvidsson/Tiofoto: 53 br. Kenneth Bengtsson/Naturbild: 50 /5, 79 tl, 79 br. Staffan Brundell/Great Shots: 18 t. Dick Clevestam/Naturbild: 94 b. Lars Dahlström/Tiofoto: 46, 66-67, 69 t+b, 72 t, 72-73, 100 b. Per Domeij: 111. Anders Ekholm/Tiofoto: 50 /1, 51, 59, 81b, 90-91, 111. Peter Gerdehag/Great Shots: 18 b, 22, 23, 25, 26-27, 29 t+b, 44-45, 50/3, 68-69, 74-75, 83, 84-85, 92. Christer Hallgren: 44 b. Sven Halling/Naturbild: 102 t. Hans Hammarskiöld/Tiofoto: 54. Bengt Hedberg/-Naturbild: 51, 76, 79 tr. Jan Peter Lahall/Great Shots: 46-47, 92-93, 95. Peter Lilja/Great Shots: 77. Nationalmuseum: 66, 72 b. Tero Niemi/Naturbild: 50/2. Pressens Bild: 111. Jan Rietz/Tiofoto: 53 tl. Magnus Rietz: 4, 7, 8-9, 10, 12-13, 14, 15, 16, 17, 19, 20-21, 24-25, 28, 30, 31 bl, 34, 35, 36-37, 38-39, 40-41, 42-43, 49, 50/6, 52, 53 tr, 55, 56, 57, 58, 60-61, 64-65, 82, 96 t+b, 98, 99 b, 101, 102 b, 106, 107 t, 107 bl, 111. Anders Rising/Tiofoto: 62, 63, 107 br, 109 . Pierre Rosberg/Tiofoto: 27. Stefan Rosengren/-Naturbild: 108 b. Sven Rosenhall/Great Shots: 31 tl, tr, br, 44 t, 50/4. Ulf Sjöstedt/Tiofoto: 48. Hans Strand/Great Shots: 5, 6-7, 8, 11, 32-33, 78, 80, 81 t, 88-89, 94 t, 99 t, 103, 104-105, 111. Lars Thulin: 85 t+l, 89. Kurt Wästfelt: 86, 87. Lars Åström/Tiofoto: 100 t. Stefan Örtenblad/Naturbild: 79 bl.

© EGMONT BØKER FREDHØI AS – SFG, N-0055 OSLO, TEL: +47 22 47 11 50 · FAX: +47 22 47 11 74
E-MAIL: SFG@EGMONT.NO · INTERNET: WWW.TOURISTBOOKS.COM
PUBLISHED IN SWEDEN BY EGMONT RICHTER AB, S-20575 MALMÖ
TEL: +46 40 38 06 00 · FAX: +46 40 93 37 08
EVERY EFFORT HAS BEEN MADE TO TRACE COPYRIGHT HOLDERS, BUT IF ANY HAVE BEEN OVERLOOKED,
THE PUBLISHER WILL BE PLEASED TO MAKE THE NECCESSARY ARRANGEMENTS AT THE FIRST OPPORTUNITY.
THIS UNIQUE COVER DESIGN IS RECOGNISED THROUGHOUT THE WORLD.
IT IS YOUR GUARANTEE OF QUALITY. ACCEPT NO IMITATIONS.
PRINTED BY NØRHAVEN A/S, DENMARK

Also available:

DESTINATIONS COLLECTION

The Best of Norway

Languages:

English
German
French
Dutch
Portuguese
Chinese
Finnish
Norwegian
Italian
Spanish
Russian
Japanese
Korean

CLASSIC COLLECTION

Norway – incl. CD

Languages:

English
German
Spanish
Japanese
Norwegian
French
Italian
Russian

A Taste of Norway

Languages:

Norwegian
English
German
French

Th. Kittelsen: Trolls

Languages:

English
German
Spanish
Japanese
Norwegian
French
Italian
Dutch

HISTORY COLLECTION

The Vikings

Languages:

English
German
Italian
Spanish
Swedish
Icelandic
Norwegian
Japanese
French
Dutch
Danish
Russian

Viking Cookbook

Languages:

English
Spanish
Norwegian
German
French
Danish

CHILDREN'S COLLECTION

Magnus Viking

Languages:

Norwegian
German
French
English
Spanish
Danish
Swedish

Elgar

Languages:

Norwegian
German
French
English
Spanish
Swedish

The Little Troll

Languages:

Norwegian
German
Spanish
Japanese
Swedish
English
French
Italian
Dutch

VIDEO COLLECTION

The Best of Norway

Format:	*Languages:*
VHS/PAL	English
VHS/NTSC	American
VHS/PAL	Norwegian
VHS/PAL	German
VHS/NTSC	Japanese
VHS/PAL	Italian
VHS/SECAM	French
VHS/PAL	Spanish
VHS/NTSC	Spanish
VHS/PAL	Korean

If your local retailer does not stock our titles, please visit our web site: www.touristbooks.com